Echoes of Insanity

Ashley Klimowicz

BookLeaf Publishing

India | USA | UK

Presentation by *BookLeaf Publishing*

Web: www.bookleafpub.com

E-mail: info@bookleafpub.com

ISBN: 9789360949204

First edition 2024

To those who have always told me to keep writing and who have supported me without pause.

PREFACE

Please read with care. Mental illness isn't shy about how it harms those it touches. Some possibly triggering content.

Echoes

Echoes through the haze -
A violent, vicious victory.
Clawing at the words;
heart racing.
Falling
faster,
faster,
faster.
Can you feel it?
Can you hear it?
As the noise absconds with your sanity
do you know where you are?
Warmth underneath.
Clammy skin.
Maniacal laughter.
Visions you can't describe.
Faster.
Breathing faster.
The thunder is in your ears.

Fighting imaginary monsters.
Throat raw, ragged breaths.
The nightmare is your reality.
Perpetual terror.
Is this the truth?
Is it a lie?
Slowly,
slowly,
Wake up. Wake up.
No one the wiser of your terror.

Beautifully Scarred

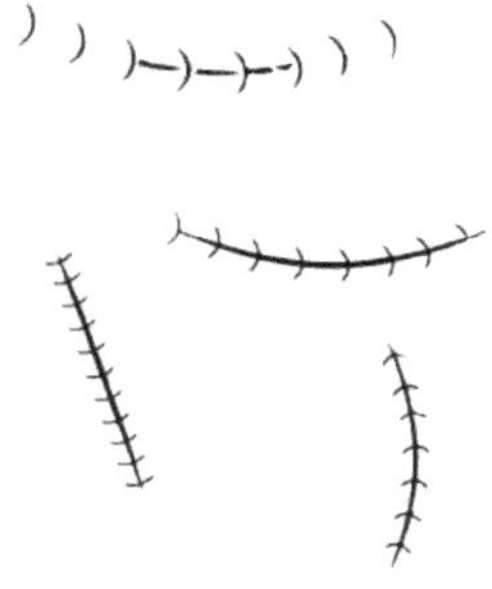

The first time we sat together,
just you and I,
I rolled up my sleeves to show you
the secrets I kept hidden there.
My nerves were going haywire,
and I felt sick to my stomach.
You looked and you scanned
the rows of scars across my arms.
I never spoke of them directly,
but I told you I was lost once;
Lost to myself and everyone around.
I told you there were things I did
just to survive myself.
You never spoke,
but you traced the reminders.
Your fingers trailed across the rigid flesh.
Even with the deformities -
In your eyes I am still beautiful.

Lost Innocence

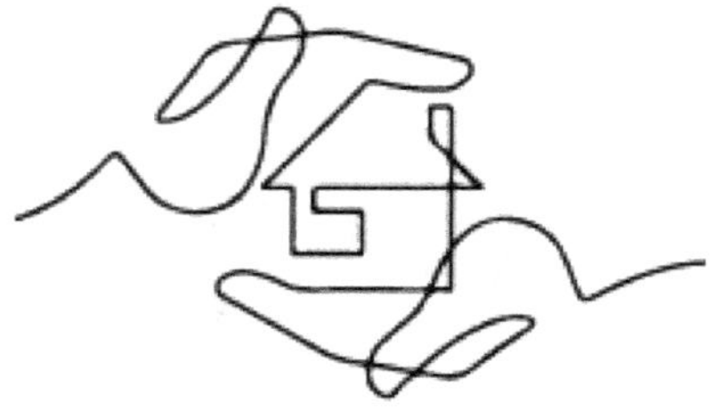

Voices loud and violent
echo around the chamber.
Trapped.
It's dark.
The wind is howling
through broken windows -
melodious and haunting.
Alone.
Barely alive.
They do not care.
Compliant.
Obedient.
Malleable.
Broken.
Beg for drugs to sleep,
to numb the agonizing pain.
Not this time.
Awake and silent; taken.
Another building - another home.

Yet, these places are not safe.
There is no love here -
just lust.
For a child barely a woman,
for another lost to the void.

Shards of Life

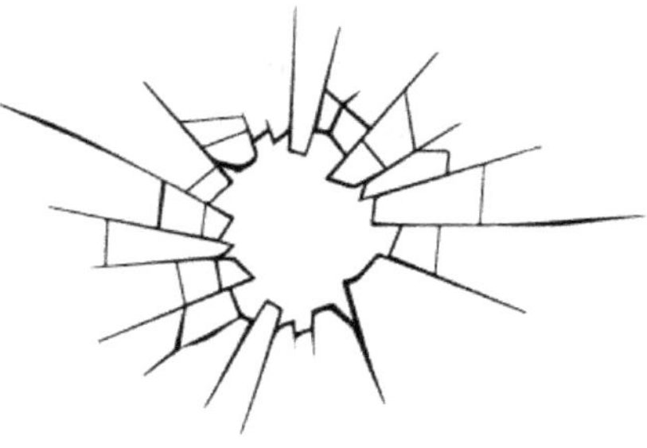

With fingers soft
as new baby skin
you trail them across my chest.
Your whisper;
light as smoke
       billowing
through the
          wind.
Shockwaves of sparkling joy
cascade through my body.
But this body is not only mine.
I am not only yours.
Fragmented shards
of a once delicately crafted plate -
shattered by the tides of time.
We are but wisps,
clinging to life
like a ghost remembers;
tendrils of a time once lived.

Ghosts

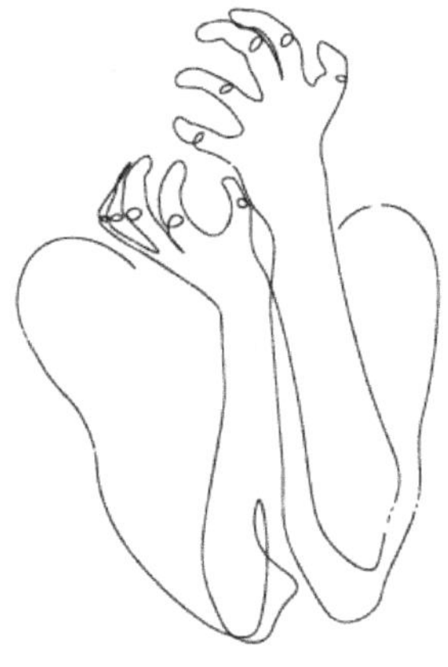

a ghost of a whisper crosses her lips
Tendrils of a plea; escape -
help me.
but then the wind howls.
the floor falls out from underneath,
taking with it the breath from her lungs.
in the blackness surrounding
voices chant, rhythmic and haunting:
speak, speak, speak.
she opens her mouth to scream it out,
bleed out the monster she has buried so deep.
but nothing pours out, but gasps for air that
aren't coming.
the foundation crumbles,

and she falls deeper, darker.
"speak now, speak, scream," chant the voices.
help me, please help.
but there's no sound, just glimpses of safety -
unattainable.
a light that she craves, but cannot hold
because it never stays.
the void of darkness opens again,
mocking the stitches through her lips.
speak up, speak louder, why aren't you
speaking?
and as she tries to rip them out
those above push her further below.

Remnants

"Take it off, baby
you're a star, you're a star!
Let's see it all, darling
isn't this what you want?"
I want to bleach my insides
Rip off my skin
Bathe in lava
And never speak again.
I want to burn the places
Your hands touched.
I want to scream and scream
Until I can't talk.
You tore me apart,
Left my blood on your chest.

Broke down my guard
Until there was nothing left.
"But you didn't fight back,
you liked it, I saw it.
That look in your eyes"
It was fear
It was terror
It was my fucking demise.
Yet your movements kept going,
Aren't you satisfied yet?
Silence isn't consent,
with your hands 'round my neck.
can I even speak or fight you back?
Yet, you kept going
and now there's nothing left -
Of my mind, of my heart.
Just self-loathing and hate.
Feelings YOU should feel,
yet I'm left broken; a mess.
Picking up more shattered pieces
of my soul, so scared and lonely.
When does it stop?
When will it end?

Lost in Limbo

If I screamed
Could you hear me?
Would you reach your hand
And grasp mine;
carry me to safety?
Or would you laugh,
Grin and smirk?
Watch me as I suffer?
Bleeding out;
Ripped to shreds from the inside
So much hatred coursing through
My open veins
How can I love myself
When no one else loves me?
How can I save myself
When the world is deadly?

Safer alone,
But crushed by loneliness.
Happier together,
Yet terrified you'll leave.
Stuck in a limbo
I wouldn't wish on anyone.

Light in the Darkness

Somewhere through the static,
Through the screams and internal cries,
Lies a child, silenced by a hand on her throat.
Inside she's screaming and begging
for the dirty, soiled floor
Full of years of blood and tears,
To swallow her broken, bleeding body
Down into the depths of hell.
For surely fire and brimstone
Feels better than he does
As he rips her to shreds.

Fingernails indent the wood -
Releasing the sounds
She's forbidden to make.
Conditioned for silence;
Conditioned for pain.

She closes her eyes and dreams.
Escapes to a place
Full of magic and love and warmth.
Where his calloused hands can't reach.
Where a fairy holds her hand
And whispers "I love you."
And the sun burns out the darkness.
"I love you too."

Velvet Masquerade

In the dark it's quiet.
There's no sound beneath the velvet;
That loving, suffocating cloak.
Where hands can't reach to harm
and words can't reach to heal.
That blackness breeds despair -
ghoulish fingers of dread
wrapping around the soft throats of the innocent.
Where obscurity brings on comfort,
and a warm, thick embrace of invisibility.
To cleave the veil is to break the spell;
A curse, yet blessing of a masquerade.
It's not safe to leave, yet more dangerous to stay.
To be alone is crushing.
To be together is unimaginable.
And so we float,
lost to the sound of the inescapable -
the inexcusable.

Hourglass

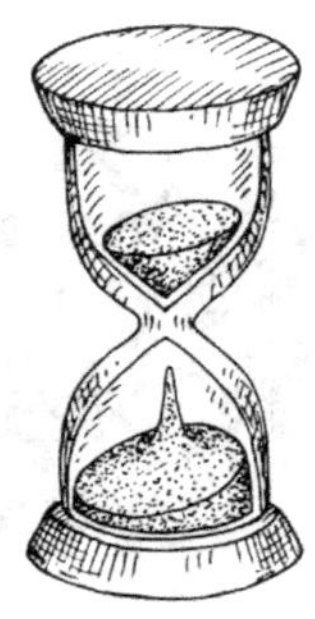

Freckled starlight lingers overhead,
those star-shaped refugees a long way from
home.
the wind howls its agonizing song as
apologies and lost souls drift on the tendrils of
another day.
shaky feet planted at the precipe of
hopelessness, daring themselves to jump.
to dive into the blackness is to dive into despair -
the cold, sharp sting of lost dreams.
no safety net awaits.
the walls of your cell are barbed and cracked,
spewing vitriol and falsehoods.
but it's a comfortable hate.
The sharp edges become dull
And the words become truths
Spilling into your every intention.

The light of the sun, the glimmer of the stars -
too bright; too kind.
The warmth of their glow feels like lava,
scalding your worn flesh.
They beckon you to love, to accept forgiveness.
But the wind screams again, the black,
death-like hands draw you into their embrace.
Another day, whispers the light.
Another day, mocks the darkness.
and the hourglass of life ticks on.

Dissociation

Static, buzzing foamy static
Bones feel hollow, head is fire
Internal, external, voices are crushing
Speaking, screaming
Numb but feeling the weight of
Hands, words, memories
Heavy
Heavier
Suffocating
trying to breathe but there's no air
Shaking, fuzzy, confused
Block it, stop it, close your ears
Clench your fists, your jaw
Beg to end it all
Then
Silence, blissful, agonizing silence.

Ruined

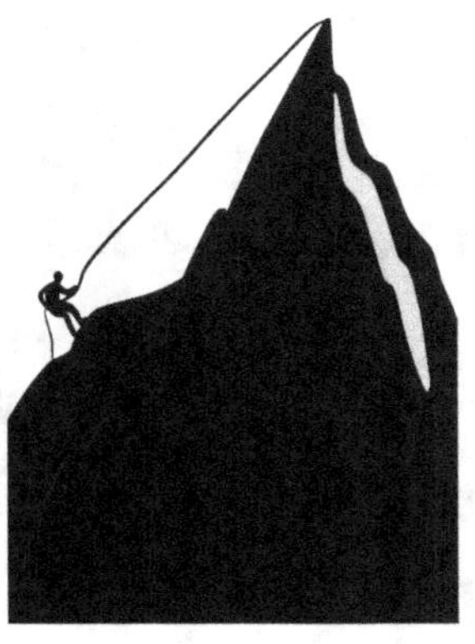

There is no quiet, no tranquility, no peace.
Chaos blows in and out,
Not bearing witness to the devastation;
The ruin it leaves in its wake.
And the screams don't end.
They echo around,
shards replicating the past.
Over and over and over
Stabbing out in anger, in pain, in sadness.
Clotted, fuzzy, broken memories,
Mixing with shattered dreams.
Drowning under their weight
And suffocating beneath forced platitudes.
There is no strength in lies,
There is no safety in strength.
Yet still, we march.

Happy

It looms above us;
The ever-elusive "happy."
We claw at the walls of our hole with
Fingernails torn and bloody.
Screaming to the wind -
Begging for an escape.
The wind laughs and blusters,
Stirring up caked-on dust and grime.
Choking and gasping,
We try, try again.
One step forward,
Thirty steps backward.
The mud and memories

Leaves us dirty and battered.
There's a cold that doesn't warm,
And a fire that won't burn.
Hiding behind the cracks,
is the darkness,
the depth of despair -
That the light touches
But doesn't permeate.
"Happy" dances and calls out,
Showing us where the black lives within.
Sleep beckons us to the comfortable ease,
Resigned to our hole.
Hopeless and lost
As "happy" walks away, once more.

The Climb

I climb up the mountain,
My feet bruised and bloody.
Marching to the beat
Of agonizing dissociation.
Of internal violence
Preceded by external silence.
They throw rocks and boulders;
Crushing me beneath the weight.
Burying me under piles of obscurity.
Erasing my voice as I beg for help.
Telling me to climb, climb, CLIMB
Do not stop, do not weep.
Unsteady, I limp,
the weight too heavy to hold.
Am I a person?
Or an appendage to fulfill others' happiness?
Do I matter?
Or do I live only for others to use?
Over and over again I am crushed,
Yet I must continue.
When is it enough?
When am I enough?

Man on the Ledge

You're standing on a ledge
feet hanging over the edge.
Life's decisions come back,
haunting you and judging you.
Time flies by.
Minutes turn to hours;
hours turn to days.
It stops for no one.
Memories come back of
past deeds, past greed.
Is this it?
You are completely alone.
Not a single thing will follow you
into this precipice.
Everyone is waiting,
there's no turning back.
Jump.

Imaginary Child

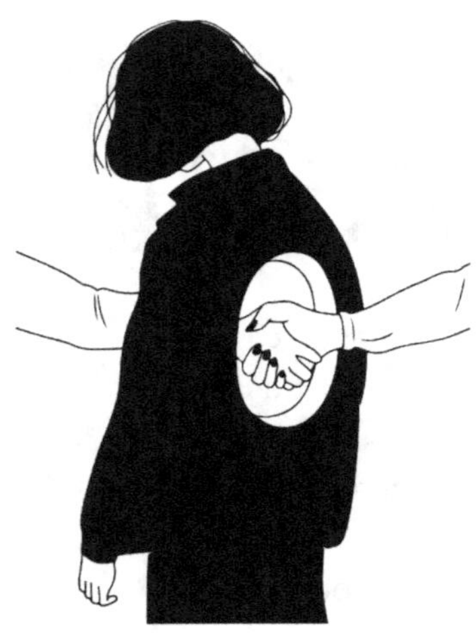

There was a fire in your eyes
in the beginning;
A scream in your voice,
but you were never heard.
"Nobody cares."
They always informed you.
You were the imaginary child,
always fading into the background.
You waded through life
barely half-alive.
But one night you called out,
breaking your silence.
It was too late,

your decision already made.
Mom and dad ran,
finally realizing your sadness.
But you were already gone.
Then everyone knew you-
your achievements and goals.
They mourned, but soon you were forgotten.
You were the imaginary child,
evaporated from memory.

Fly Away

Where are you?
Is it beautiful?
Are you beautiful?
Take me away.
I want to be lovely too.
Is it everything we believed?
Can you even see me?
Are you watching over me?
Am I living up to everything
you expected of me?
Take me with you.
I want to watch too.
Can you fly
with blinding white wings
and a halo on your head?
Are you alone?
Take me with you.
I want to fly too.

Cracked

You're trying to build
on something that's breaking down.
There're cracks in the foundations
of what was once a magnificent palace.
Our love once the glue holding us together.
Now it's dried up, musty and dirty,
leaving our feelings blowing in the wind.
What was once a beautiful feeling
now lay dead and cold on the ground.
Our bliss evaporated,

replaced by jealousy and hate.
Where did we go wrong?
When did it become normal to feel so
alone?
The tears and the screaming,
your eyes dull and lackluster.
You cracked through my walls
left a storm in my home,
then left, fixing the wall you broke.
But even things mended will never
return to the same glamor they once held.

Helpless

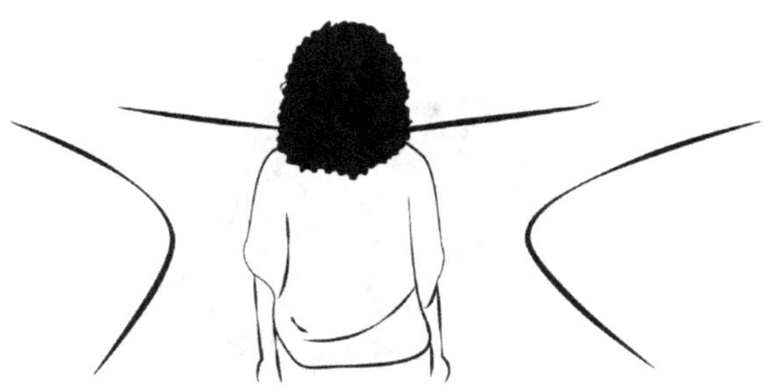

There you lie,
body sprawled across the floor.
Tattered, scattered, ripped up pieces;
Addicted so helplessly.
Your veins flood with poison,
Your lungs fill with smoke.
Those promises break easy,
Don't they?
When you're left out alone?
Who's your friend, in that place
Of horrors and nightmares?
Nobody but the drugs you need,
And the other dead bodies
Whose skin's just like yours;
Pale white-paper thin.
No life left in those eyes;
Mind's blank since the end
Of the life you once lived.

Shattered Glass

Who am I to keep fighting?
To hold onto something that's
crumbling beneath my fingertips?
I'm not the strong girl I was.
My soul aches for a break,
to be happy in complete solitude.
But there is no light
at the end of this tunnel.

Happiness was once on my doorstep,
begging for me to come outside.
But I slammed the door and locked it.
Instead of leaving,
I released my inner demons.
They taunt me and remind me that I am weak.

I can't resist the urge
to carve my pain into my skin.
I can't seem to look away as
the rushing blood stains my sheets.

Who am I?
Certainly not a soldier, fighting to survive.
My gun has been broken and ruined.
Certainly not an innocent girl
who lacks the knowledge to carry on.
I am stuck in complacency,
willing to accept my fate instead of change it.

I feel empty and hopeless,
praying for the day happiness returns.
And instead of knocking,
it kicks my door down and steals my soul
before this darkness overwhelms me.

Alone

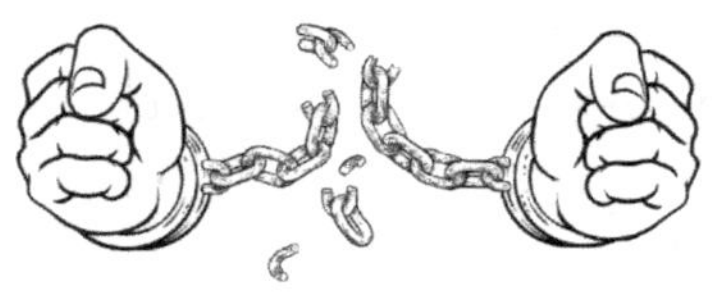

Bones cracked beneath her feet;
White daggers shining
Like marrow in the cold night.
The silence was static
Her racing heart slicing through
Like a knife wrapped in poison.
There was no direction,
Nothing except the hand of terror
Gripping her insides.
Twisting and turning,
Guiding her wayward body.
"Come home,"
Cooed the voice,
Malice dripping from each sound
Like blood against a tile floor.
Home?
There is no home.
Just the growing darkness,
The cooling night,
And her broken, reeling mind.

Death

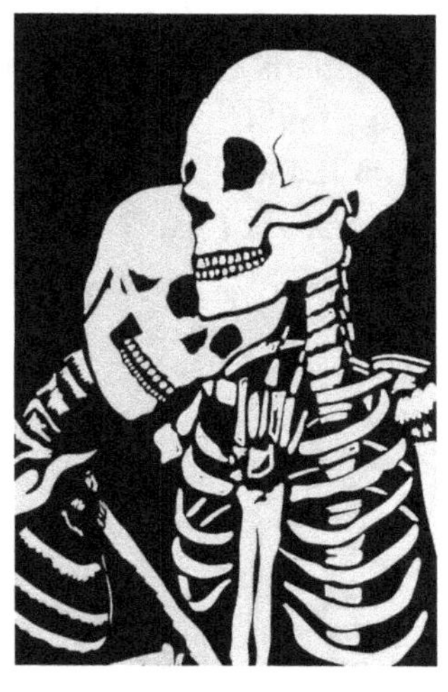

If I died tonight,
What would tomorrow look like?
Would there be anger or grief?
Would there be candles lit and
tearful speeches given?
Or would there be blame while
hatred coursed through their veins,
shaming and blaming
my overwhelming decision?
Would time march onward,
Forever ticking; an eternal sound?
Or would it pause,
enveloping those closest
in a red cloud of agony?

As my body became one with the earth,
Would anyone miss me?
As worms ate out my insides,
Would anyone remember me?
Or are we all lost in this
Cacophony of hurt and fear
Connected by tendrils of pain?

Crippled Heart

The waves crash above me
I'm drowning I'm drowning.
But there's no one here
To take the rocks from my ankles.
I try to hold my breath,
Swim to the surface and gasp.
But the weight pulls me under
Again and again and again.
Words flood my thoughts:
"You're faking"
"Attention seeking"
"You're a liar"
The blue is all-encompassing
The deep doesn't release survivors.
I'll go down to the bottom
I'll make peace with the dark.
Because that's what happens
When the hurt cripples your heart.

Absolute Isolation

Have you ever felt alone in a crowded room?
Been surrounded by friends and lovers,
but yet an emptiness still sits in your chest?
Have you ever laughed, or smiled,
but felt the tears well up when you close your
eyes?
Have you ever felt isolated,
while the whole room is held together?
Forgotten about and taken away
to a place where your heart knows some
companionship?
Flicking out the ashes of your cigarette,
knowing each breath might be your last?
Have you ever listened to the sympathy,
but retained none of it?
Your mind remains blank and distorted.
The pain of past problems and demands
rises to the surface bringing new sorrows.
So you sit, writing out a new poem or story,

trying to figure out what's going wrong.
Where you went wrong.
Everything is always wrong.

The World

Happy endings are obsolete.
All of these fairytales are lying.
Their half-assed stories are giving us false hope.
What's there to smile about?
We live in a world where money overpowers
love.
Where a kid will get killed
for the dirt bike she rode on.
We've forgotten where we've come from.
But everyone's rushing,
and trying to move forward.
We look to the future
instead of thinking about our past.
While they don't define us,
they created us.
But we hide them and conceal them;
skeletons are meant to stay dead.
But they're there, dancing and smiling.
Waiting until you slip up.

They'll come falling out of
your picture-perfect life.
And who will be there to
push them back in?
The monsters are under your bed
and in your head.
They creep into your closet
and inside of your heart.
But you'll close your eyes
to block out the demons.
One world full of
close-minded, blind individuals.
They'll turn their heads to the violence.
We're desensitized.
A media-fueled aggressive culture.
Nothing can change,
one will always hate.
Happily ever after is full of shit
in this fucked up story we live in.

Anguish

I stand alone,
wind blowing around me
at the end of my time.
A shattered being
that at some point had resembled a human.

The sky is black and
scattered stars light up the world around me.
How could such a beautiful world
bring so much agony?

I am so completely alone.
Water rushes across my feet;
a sign that the tide is rising.

How peaceful it would be
to become one with the waves.
How lovely it would be
to never hurt again.

I'm standing here screaming
'Please, God, take my life.'
But he isn't listening.
So I rip at my flesh and
beckon sweet death.
But it does not arrive.

How am I meant to survive
with nothing left to fight for?
I can smile and make believe,
but my eyes are dead.

As I watch the stars twinkle above me,
I close my eyes and breathe, whispering
'Death, come to me.'

Bottom of a Bottle

You live at the bottom of a bottle,
your life supply not the air you breathe,
but the drugs you ingest.
The pills, the powders,
trapping you in a permanent haze.
You're stuck.
The alcohol your only friend.
When does it stop?
Is the pain too steep?
Agony seeps into your veins.

Malicious intent creeping through your daily
turmoils.
Your future is bleak.
Inner pain ripping you to shreds.
You self-medicate, but it'll never stop.
There is only one way out.
It was all too much.
Another life lost to the monsters in the closet.

Torture

Some say that
"depression doesn't need a reason."
That sometimes your brain is
"a mess of mixed signals."
I don't want a broken brain,
or one destroyed by repressed memories.
Where one day I'll wake up,
happy and cheerful and my silly self.
And then it comes crashing down,
like a brick to my chest.

I'll have another panic attack,
tears forcing their way to my eyes.
I'll freak out and scream and rant and rave
until I no longer know who I am.
Not like I fucking know who I am anyway.

I feel like a monster;
a creature hiding inside the ugly flesh of a
human.
I can't be alone for more than 20 minutes
without my thoughts running wild.
Who would miss me if I was gone?
What are the consequences?
But I'm happy, right?
I'm the happiest girl alive.
I made promises.
I promise to never cut again
I won't smoke pot
I'll quit the cigarettes.
But that slow inhale and exhale frees me.
I exhale the hatred for myself
for a father who won't love me
and for a man who took everything.
Who robbed me of a youth that was promising.
I was smart, I could do it.
But how can you study
when the needle calls your name?
Or when you're hooked up to IVs
pumping life into your veins?

I'm "weak" because I self-medicate,
and being depressed is "sickening".
I don't want this fucking brain anyway.
You can have my thoughts,

or the paralyzing flashbacks.
You can take the agonizing anxiety,
and the self-hatred.
I just want it to end
before I lose it completely.

www.ingramcontent.com/pod-product-compliance
Lightning Source LLC
Chambersburg PA
CBHW061722130726
47996CB00006B/2452